American Quilt

CLASSICS
1800 • 1980

The Bresler Collection

Kristen S. Watts

EDITOR

Mint Museum of Craft + Design
Charlotte, North Carolina

The Mint Museums
Experience art

This catalog is published on the occasion of the exhibition
American Quilt Classics, 1800-1980: The Bresler Collection
organized by the Mint Museum of Craft + Design, Charlotte, North Carolina.

EXHIBITION DATES
August 30, 2003 through January 4, 2004

Kristen S. Watts, *Project Manager and Editor*
Melissa G. Post, *Curator and Editor*
Mark R. Leach, *Deputy Director*
Merikay Waldvogel, *Essayist*
Mary Beth Ausman, *Education Resource Coordinator*
Charles L. Mo, *Chief Curator*
Emily Blanchard, *Graphic Designer*
Kurt Warnke, *Exhibition Designer*
Martha T. Mayberry, *Registrar*
Katherine Stocker, *Associate Registrar*
David H. Ramsey, *Photographer*
Beth McLaughlin, *Textile Conservator*
Kari Hayes, *Conservation Seamstress*

Copyright © 2003 Mint Museum of Craft + Design
All rights reserved. No part of this publication may be used without the express written permission
from the Mint Museum of Craft + Design.

Library of Congress Cataloging-in-Publication Data

American quilt classics, 1800-1980: the Bresler collection / Kristen S. Watts, project manager.
   p. cm.
Catalog of an exhibition at the Mint Museum of Craft + Design, Aug. 30, 2003-Jan. 4, 2004. Includes biblio-
graphical references. 1. Quilts—United States—Exhibitions. 2. Bresler, Fleur—Art collections—Exhibitions. 3.
Quilts—North Carolina—Charlotte—Exhibitions. 4. Mint Museum of Craft + Design—Exhibitions. I. Watts,
Kristen S. II. Mint Museum of Craft + Design.
  NK9112.A538 2003
  746.46'0973'07475676—dc22

2003015634

*Funding for this publication and exhibition generously provided by the Founders' Circle Ltd.,
the national support affiliate of the Mint Museum of Craft + Design.*

*The Mint Museums receive operating support from the Arts & Science Council-
Charlotte/Mecklenburg, Inc.; the North Carolina Arts Council, an agency funded by the
State of North Carolina and the National Endowment for the Arts; the City of Charlotte;
and their members.*

CONTENTS

ACKNOWLEDGMENTS
Kristen S. Watts

American Quilt Classics, 1800-1980: The Bresler Collection would not have been realized without the help of many dedicated people. First and foremost, I extend my sincerest thanks to Fleur and Charles Bresler. Between 2000 and 2001, the Breslers donated 36 historically significant American quilts along with books and research materials to the Mint Museum of Craft + Design. Their gift, celebrated in this exhibition and catalog, will serve as a foundation for an American textiles collection at the museum.

I also gratefully acknowledge the continued generous support of the Founders' Circle, the national affiliate of the Mint Museum of Craft + Design, which enabled the museum to publish this beautiful catalog.

My work on this project would have been impossible without the assistance, on-going support, humor and patience of the Mint Museums' staff. Several staff members contributed significantly to this project. Mark Leach, Deputy Director of the Mint Museums, worked closely with the Breslers from their initial donation. His artistic vision inspires me and paved the way for a gift of this magnitude. Chief Curator Charles Mo's experience and professional guidance greatly assisted me on this project.

Curator Melissa Post worked closely with me on this project. Melissa generously gave her time to help edit the catalog and patiently answered all my questions. I am grateful to have Melissa as a mentor. Education Resource Coordinator Mary Beth Ausman also assisted this project through her editing skills, ability to think out-of-the-box, and friendship.

Registrar Martha Tonissen Mayberry and Associate Registrar Katherine Stocker cataloged and conditioned the quilts upon their arrival at the museum. Katherine also worked closely with me on the conservation and photography of the quilts. Katherine's sense of humor and friendship helped me throughout this project.

I am also grateful to the entire Design and Installation Department who approach each project of the Mint Museums with fresh, creative ideas. Graphic Designer Emily Blanchard designed this catalog as well as exhibition graphics and advertisements for *American Quilt Classics*. Kurt Warnke, Head of Design and Installation, worked with me to develop an innovative layout for the exhibition. Chief Preparator Mitch Francis, Preparator Leah Blackburn, and Preparator William Lipscomb expertly installed the quilts. The creativity and skill of the entire department never ceases to amaze me.

I extend my sincerest appreciation to those people at the core of the museum's daily operations: Executive Director Phil Kline, Chief Financial Officer Mike Smith, Information Technology Manager John West, Accountants Hannah Pickering and Lois Schneider, Facilities Manager Ed Benton, and the Security and Front Desk Staffs. My sincerest thanks also go to Anna Sims, Assistant to the Deputy Director and Founders Circle Coordinator, for her talent and her boundless energy.

A handful of persons outside of the museum also contributed to the success of this project. Photographer David Ramsey, as always, sensitively photographed the 36 quilts in the collection. The Mint Museums are fortunate have a long-standing relationship with David. Beth McLaughlin, Textile Conservator, and Kari Hayes, Conservation Seamstress, worked to properly preserve and ensure the safe presentation of the quilts. I also thank Quilt Historian Merikay Waldvogel for the passion and effort she put into writing about the Bresler Collection against the backdrop of quilting history.

And, finally, my family and friends deserve innumerable thanks. My husband Jody's encouragement, love and friendship enable me to undertake projects such as this. For their unfailing belief in me, I thank Mary Davidson, Dawn Davidson, Tucker and Kym Davidson, as well as Ethel King, Zinnia Willits, and Jenelle Edick.

Birds and Butterflies Quilt (detail)

We think of quilts as providing physical warmth. Warmth may come in more than one guise. The Bresler Quilt Collection is the result of a very personal vision. It was not assembled with the aid of a curator. Rather, I collected what appealed to me and what gave me a feeling of warmth. My husband and my family lived with, enjoyed, and utilized these quilts for many years. More than two-thirds of these quilts were always on view in our home. They hung on our walls, covered our beds, and were lovingly draped over antique quilt racks. Grandchildren, family, and visitors alike loved, admired, and used these quilts and were comforted by them.

Over the past few years, these quilts have become part of the permanent collection of the Mint Museum of Craft + Design. Though they are missed, we feel that they have gone to a better place. It is our greatest hope and desire that these quilts will continue to be a source of beauty and inspiration, creativity and comfort to many people. We are pleased by the educational and outreach programs organized by the Mint Museum of Craft + Design. By placing these quilts on the museum's website they will be reaching an even broader audience, one interested in research and examination. We hope that this exhibition will bring children and families together and provide them with enjoyment, appreciation, and knowledge. We wish to thank Mark Leach, the staff of the museum, and all of the others who toiled to bring this exhibition to fruition and to document our collection with this beautiful catalog.

Fleur Bresler and the Bresler Family

Medallion Quilt (detail)

*T*wenty-five years ago, one quilt changed my life. Obviously something similar happened to Fleur Bresler, who collected the quilts you are about to see. Printed fabrics enthralled her. Quirky appliqué designs tickled her fancy. The Amish quilts spoke to her. Over a quarter of a century, Fleur Bresler's personal hobby evolved into a passion to learn all there was to know about quilts—inside and out.

In a telephone conversation with Fleur, I learned that she grew up with no quilts in her family. Her first quilt was a kelly green and white Double Wedding Ring, for which she paid $30 in 1971. She remembers it fondly, "It was machine-pieced and hand-quilted. I found it visually appealing. My daughter Sue took it to college and returned it four years later in shreds."[1]

Invited by a friend to attend a quilting group, Fleur was not intimidated by the hand quilting the group prescribed. "I sewed as a child—made doll clothes, etc. I even had a grand idea to make a quilt for each of my six children. My oldest daughter, now an adult and mother herself, just received a Boston Commons Quilt last year. I decided long ago it would be simpler and faster to collect quilts than to make them by hand."

In July 1978, Fleur traveled over 1000 miles to the Kansas Quilt Symposium in Lawrence, one of the first quilt events to attract quilt enthusiasts from across the nation. There, quilting instructors gave workshops while quilt historians lectured and shared patterns. New quilts were also on display. Fleur bought a Hawaiian appliqué quilt on peach and dark blue print fabric. Never intending to use it, Fleur instead displayed her contemporary quilt in the foyer of her apartment.

Fleur's interest in antique quilts was sparked by her volunteer work at the

National Museum of American History at the Smithsonian. Doris Bowman, Curator of the Textile Collection, encouraged docents to research quilts in the collection. During her tenure as a docent, Fleur led a weekly behind-the-scenes tour of the quilt collection and researched all-white quilts, indigo resist fabrics, glazed wool quilts, printed chintzes, and commemorative handkerchiefs. She became familiar with the work of textile and quilt historians Barbara Brackman, Florence Montgomery, Florence Pettit, and Patsy Orlofsky and assembled her own library of quilt and textile history books. She also befriended Stella Rubin, a nationally known collector and dealer of antique quilts. Such recognized and respected figures indirectly shaped the formation of the Bresler Quilt Collection. Fleur explained, "This was my education and the impetus for my quilt collecting. It opened my eyes to the possibility of creating a small representative group of quilts with historical significance."

In 2000, Fleur donated the bulk of her quilt collection, which spanned nearly 200 years, as well as her books and research materials to the Mint Museum of Craft + Design. Fleur expressed her hopes, "As a collector you collect for your own pleasure and enjoyment, but a part of you wants to share your passion with other people. The collection is small, but needed to remain intact because of its historical content. There was a genuine and immediate need for this material at the new museum for both display and study purposes."

Keeping Fleur's hopes in mind, the following essay explores the historical context and significance of the quilts in the Bresler Collection in order to foster a deeper understanding and appreciation for the work.

I extend my personal appreciation to Fleur Bresler and to Mark Leach, Deputy Director for the Mint Museums, for inviting me to study these quilts so closely.

Merikay Waldvogel
QUILT HISTORIAN

The Evolution of the American Quilt

The American quilt has been called the quintessential metaphor for the American experience. Layered, stitched, embellished, and re-worked, quilts reflect the cultural, aesthetic and artistic heritage of this country. Quilts have never been simple, utilitarian bedcovers; too much time and imagination goes into making a quilt for its purpose to overshadow its creative form. When one studies American quilts, one comes face to face with the nation's history, its people, and their cultural development.

The first colonists arrived with quilted bed coverings and centuries-old needlework traditions. However, these traditions were quickly adapted to accommodate and reflect life first in the colonies then in the young nation. New printing technology made brighter, less expensive fabrics available. With the onset of wars and economic crises, the desire for imported fabrics waned as the need for domestic fabrics increased. Together, these factors contributed to the evolution of the America quilt. By the mid-1800s, an American style emerged that was distinct from its British and European antecedents. Succeeding generations not only revived and reinterpreted earlier quilt designs, but also added patterns and layouts using contemporary fabrics and color schemes.

The thirty-six quilts in the Bresler Collection span nearly 200 years of quilt designs (1800-1980). Specifically, the collection includes whole cloth, white work, indigo resist and block-printed chintz quilts dating from the late eighteenth and early nineteenth centuries. It also includes examples of appliqué, stenciled, mosaic-template pieced, and album quilts from the mid-1800s as well as log cabin, crazy, and charm quilts from the late nineteenth century. Also within the collection are a handful of twentieth century quilts, some of which are slightly atypical. For example, the Amish quilts from Pennsylvania and the Midwest were made concurrently with the heady quilt revival of the 1920s and 1930s, but their reductive use of color and simplified pattern formats allude to quilts made a hundred years earlier. Call them "folk art" or "fine art," these magnificent quilts were made by artists who ventured beyond the prescribed rules and formats and bequeathed a record of their lives and the world in which they lived.

QUILTMAKING BASICS

Quiltmaking has remained essentially the same since the seventeenth century. A quilt is simply two layers of fabric stitched together with batting in between. There are three basic steps: first assembling the quilt top and backing to create the layers; next sewing, or quilting, the layers together; and, finally, finishing the quilt by binding the edges. To make a quilt top, you first choose a pattern block and layout; find appropriate fabric; or make a pattern or templates from paper, tin, sandpaper, or plastic; mark and cut the fabric; and finally sew the top and backing together. Piecing consists of sewing patches, one to another, with a running stitch, making a seam. Piecing usually results in geometric designs such as stars. Appliqué consists of sewing fabric shapes onto a contrasting background (usually white) to produce a curvilinear, floral,

or pictorial design. Quilters often combine both techniques in one quilt.

Crazy quilts and log cabin quilts are made differently from other types of quilts. A piece of cloth (about twelve inches square) serves as the foundation for both quilt blocks. Crazy quilt blocks are composed of random-sized pieces of cloth arranged and basted down to cover the entire foundation cloth. Log cabin blocks, on the other hand, are formed by sewing strips sequentially around the four sides of a small square sewn at the center of the foundation cloth. As each strip is attached, it is folded and finger-pressed in place. The process is repeated until the foundation cloth is completely covered. The pattern blocks are then joined together to form the distinctive crazy and log cabin quilt tops (fig. 1).

Whole cloth and white work quilts are not made of individual blocks, and do not have any patchwork or appliqué. Instead, as their name implies, the quilt tops are composed of entire lengths of cloth stitched together. Whole cloth quilts made from printed cloth typically do not have extravagant quilting since it would not show against the design of the fabric. White work quilts, on the other hand, provide broad expanses of open space to showcase elaborate quilting, cording and stuffing.

The structure and design of a quilt allows for innovation and experimentation. The *Nine Patch Quilt with Stencil* in the Bresler Collection illustrates how one quilt often includes several styles, techniques, and ornamentation, such as stenciling, painting, embroidery or even beading (fig.2).

ENGLISH ROOTS OF AMERICA'S QUILTS: WHOLE CLOTH, WHITE WORK, AND MOSAIC

Figure 2
UNKNOWN ARTIST
Nine Patch Quilt and Stencil circa 1830
hand-pieced, quilted, appliquéd, and stenciled cotton
Gift of Fleur and Charles Bresler.
2000.62.5

During the seventeenth and eighteenth centuries, the American colonies provided a protected marketplace for English textile manufacturers and trading companies. Chintz fabrics imported from India and some actually printed in England in imitation of Indian textiles were popular for quilts, coverlets, and other household furnishings. Following the American Revolutionary War as textile mills were established in the United States, American women remained faithful to English decorating styles and patterns, and imported fabric was still prized.

In the Bresler Collection, there is an example of a whole cloth quilt entitled *Pillar Print Chintz Quilt,* named for the fabric from which it is constructed. It was likely made for a four-poster bed with, as dictated by English fashion, matching bed curtains, canopy and cloth-covered headboards. The pillar print chintz used in this quilt is similar to fabric printed in England in the 1830s.[2] Interestingly, there are two coverlets

Figure 3
UNKNOWN ARTIST
Resist Dye Coverlets
circa 1840
hand-pieced, quilted,
resist dyed cotton,
linen, wool, indigo dye
Gift of Fleur and
Charles Bresler.
2000.62.6.1-2

in the collection that were quite possibly cut from bed hangings. The center panel fabric in both of the indigo resist coverlets dyed with indigo using a wax-resist process, appears to be older than the border and binding fabrics (fig. 3).

Precious fabrics were often recycled to meet society's changing tastes. Whole cloth English quilts made of glazed wool (known as *calamanco*) were also present in the colonies. The wool fabric was pressed to achieve a flat surface and then a substance was applied to achieve the glossiness. The cloth may have originally been manufactured for curtains or even wall coverings, but in quilts it served as a perfect backdrop for elaborate quilting layouts containing center medallions surrounded by double plume wreaths and vines.[3]

The raised quilting on the white work quilts is known today as *trapunto* or stuffed quilting. To be precise, white work quilts employ a wide variety of techniques including cording, quilting, and stuffing as well as white-on-white embroidery and candlewicking. This particular style of quilting originated in the Mediterranean region in the seventeenth century, and became known as Marseilles quilts. One of the Bresler Quilts, the *Marseilles Crib Quilt*, is thought to have been made in France (fig. 4). Northern European and American quilters adopted this labor-intensive needlework. While it waned in Europe,

16

the style remained popular in the United States, particularly in the Southeast, until after the close of the Civil War in1865.[4]

Another example of white work in the Bresler Collection, the *Cornucopia Quilt* is quilted with fifteen stitches per inch. At the center of the quilt appears a cornucopia of stuffed flowers and leaves surrounded by a double feathered circle. American quiltmakers often dated and initialed their white work quilts. Considering how much time and skill white work quilts required, it is understandable that a quilter would want to leave her mark.

Mosaic quilts, in contrast to whole cloth quilts, are made of thousands of tiny pieces of cloth cut from print and solid fabrics. A specific piecing technique known as English Template Piecing (or English Paper Piecing) used thousands of pieces of paper that were cut and then attached to each piece of cloth in the quilt top. The maker used one master pattern (a hexagon, diamond, or square) made of tin or stiff paper to cut paper templates and then an equal number of slightly larger pieces in cloth. Cloth was then folded around and basted to each template. These cloth-covered pieces were stitched to each other with an overhand stitch. This technique, when done correctly, produces precise intersections and tight seams. With hexagon templates as small as half an inch on a side and arranged

Figure 4
UNKNOWN ARTIST
Marseilles Crib Quilt
circa 1800-1825
embroidered and quilted cotton
Gift of Fleur and Charles Bresler. 2001.38.9

17

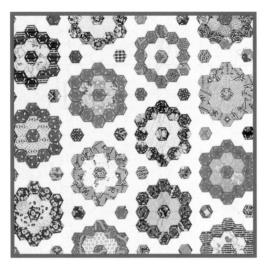

according to light and dark fabrics in rosettes, the finished effect is often dazzling, reminiscent of mosaic tile displays (fig. 5).

Though British Mosaic quilts date between the late 1700s and early 1800s, the pattern did not appear in the United States until the 1830s. The earliest known publication of the hexagon mosaic pattern in the United States is the January 1835 issue of *The Lady's Book* (later known as *Godey's Lady's Book*).[5] Paper piecing did not endure as long in the United States as it did in England and Europe. In fact, the style seems not to have spread much beyond the seaport cities along the East Coast of the United States. Very few paper template pieced quilts were made anywhere in the United States after the Civil War until the 1930s when the Honeycomb Pattern was revived as Grandmother's Flower Garden Pattern without using the paper technique.[6]

Appliqué and Album Quilts

Appliqué and *broderie perse* appliqué quilts were popular in the first half of the nineteenth century.[7] The term "appliqué" as a needlework term is derived from the French verb *appliquer*, meaning to apply or attach. Also a French expression, *broderie perse* is loosely translated as

"Persian Embroidery." This term is somewhat misleading, though, since the appliqué was not technically embroidery and the chintz fabric it employed was not directly from Persia or the Middle East. Simply, *broderie perse* refers to appliquéing individual chintz cut-outs (birds, flowers, baskets, etc.) onto a white cotton background. Quilters today prefer the term cut-out chintz appliqué.

Clever textile manufacturers, such as Philadelphia printer John Hewson, noticed of the popularity of chintz appliqué and produced pre-printed squares of floral designs and matching border prints for the quilt projects.[8] These appliqué quilts preserved pieces of chintz that otherwise would have vanished. Furthermore, the prevalence of chintz in both pieced and appliqué quilts during the nineteenth century demonstrates the close relations Americans maintained with British companies as well as the quiltmakers' respect for the fabric designs found in imported chintz.

The charm of cut-out chintz appliqué is that two quiltmakers using the same chintz print might create two very different quilts. For example, the *Broderie Perse Crib Quilt* in the Bresler Collection has a vase of flowers as a center medallion; whereas, the same printed vase was used by another quiltmaker in the four corner triangles in a full-size

Central Star Quilt made in Baltimore (fig. 6).[9]

A red-and-green floral appliqué quilt style developed during the 1840s and 1850s throughout the Mid-Atlantic and Southeastern States. The lack of available chintz fabric and the prevalence of newly introduced dyed fabrics led American quilters to develop their own appliqué designs, cutting shapes of leaves, stems, flowers and vases from appropriately colored fabrics. This new style entirely replaced the English reminiscent chintz-appliqué style by the 1860s.

Princess Feather, Coxcomb and Currants, Rose Tree, Rose of Sharon, and Whig Rose, were among the familiar names given to a portfolio of standard appliqué patterns developed during the mid-nineteenth century. A consistent layout for appliqué quilts, which emerged simultaneously, was perhaps, influenced by 1830s jacquard-woven coverlets, designed with a divided central field and a surrounding border. Four-block, six-block, and nine-block grids were common. The *Birds and Butterflies Quilt* in the Bresler Quilt Collection reflects this layout, with its six large vases surrounded by a floral border.[10]

With their sophisticated designs, precise needlework, and abundant quilting, mid-nineteenth century appliqué quilts became highly prized. They were often given as gifts to brides, newborns, and departing friends, and, thus, had names and dates embroidered, inked, or quilted onto the surface. The crib size *Medallion Quilt* in the Bresler Collection contains the nearly illegible inscription "Grandmother 1861."

In the 1840s album quilts became fashionable at the same time autograph collecting became popular. Following the introduction of non-corrosive ink suitable for writing on cloth in the mid 1830s, women inscribed their names and penned sentimental messages directly onto the fabric leaving fragile written legacies on their album quilts. Intended to commemorate events such as weddings, a minister's good works, or the birth of a child, album quilts were usually planned and coordinated by one person, while others contributed and signed the blocks. Album quilt blocks were pieced and/or appliquéd. In some cases, the same block was repeated throughout the quilt. In others, the quilt was comprised of a wide variety of blocks.[11] Particularly compelling album quilts exist in the Bresler Collection.

During the mid-1800s, album quilts varied greatly from region to region. In New York, for example, album quilts were composed of smaller blocks and had more white areas than those from other parts of the country. New Jersey album quilts often used just one block that was repeated multiple times in a grid with a surrounding border. Western Pennsylvania and Ohio versions, though similar to those of New York, were more likely to maintain the classic red-and-green color combinations of the 1850s, while Southern album quilts often included *broderie perse* appliqué blocks.

Baltimore Album quilts are regarded as the epitome of mid-nineteenth century appliqué quilts. Techniques, fabrics, and pictorial images imbue these quilts with their distinctly Baltimore flavor. Layered baskets and vases overflow with multi-colored flowers, while pictorial blocks include Baltimore monuments and buildings as well as prominent citizens, and war heroes.[12]

The Bresler Collection includes a *Baltimore Album Quilt* made by Catherine Bell Hooper (1813-1881). She was married in 1833 to

William Hooper, founder of Mount Vernon Mills, a major cotton textile mill in Baltimore. The center block features the Bible with Catherine Hooper's initials embroidered in yellow. There are no other names inscribed on the quilt and the fabrics are consistent through most of the blocks, a typical indication that the quilt was made by one person (fig. 7).

In the 1940s, Dr. William Rush Dunton Jr., a Baltimore psychiatrist, studied quilts made during the first half of the nineteenth century in Baltimore, particularly chintz appliqué and Baltimore Album quilts. His work, which included interviews with quiltmakers' descendants, technical analysis, and photography, was compiled in his 1946 book *Old Quilts*. The Catherine Bell Hooper quilt in the Bresler Collection was fully described and photographed in Dunton's book.[13]

A Unique American Style Emerges

By 1860, American styles of quiltmaking had eclipsed the preference for British medallion and mosaic style quilts. American quilters by this time used multiple blocks of equal size for both pieced and appliquéd quilts. With a ruler and compass, any geometric design was possible for pieced blocks. The fluidity of appliqué allowed for a wide range of individual creativity. While public displays of quilts at agricultural fairs allowed for the dissemination of patterns from community to community, naming of quilt patterns was informal prior to the Civil War. One pattern might be known by two different names— for example, Harrison Rose and Democratic Rose, reflecting opposing political allegiances. Biblical references, especially from the Song of Solomon, were assigned to quilt patterns, but not in any systematic way. More often than not, a quilt pattern might be called simply "Grandmother's Quilt."

The Civil War (1861-1865) radically affected the domestic life of American families. With blankets in short supply, women in the North collected thousands of quilts to keep soldiers warm. In the South, seaports were blockaded. Textile manufacturers struggled to produce cloth for tents, blankets, sheets, and hospital provisions. Women were resourceful in clothing their own families as well as their soldiers. They learned to weave cloth, knit socks, and cut up carpets for blankets.[14]

Following the war, textile mills retooled quickly and produced badly needed cloth for the domestic market. Soon low-cost printed calico was plentiful. And, for the first time, many women purchased sewing machines, which led to a revival in home sewing. Quilters, too, proudly used their machines to piece blocks, attach borders, or sew on bindings. Some even appliquéd and quilted by machine.[15]

Coincidentally, the United States Postal Service established Rural Free Delivery, putting even the most remote farm in touch with national fashions and trends. Farm and household magazines such as *Hearth and Home* of Augusta, Maine featured short stories, helpful hints, and fancy work patterns, including a monthly quilt pattern, submitted by readers. Thousands of patterns (mostly pieced) were distributed nationwide through mail order catalogs.[16] Reaching millions of subscribers throughout the country, these magazines hastened the quilting revival at the end of the nineteenth century. Quilting fads such as charm and crazy quilts may not have originated in these columns, but their popularity intensified as readers throughout the country responded to each other's queries for patterns and fabrics.

CHARM QUILTS

A charm quilt is a type of quilt in which no two patches in the quilt are cut from the same fabric. Because they needed thousands of patches for one quilt, quiltmakers went to great lengths to acquire enough cloth including placing queries in readers' columns of farm magazines.[17]

> *The Household*, May 1880
> I am making a charm quilt, and if any of the sisters will send me pieces of print four inches square, I will gladly exchange with them, on receipt of their address and size of pieces wanted.
> Florence Glidden, Holley, N.Y.

As the following entry will attest, the enthusiasm for charm quilts waned quickly for some quilters.

> *The Household*, October 1880
> The charm quilt has long ago had its day in this section. I never

knew one who undertook it but wished she was out of it. Their oddity is all the recommendation they possess. E. W. Benedict, Delaware, Ohio [18]

Charm quilts are particularly significant textile historical documents. Formed from thousands of calico print fabrics, they encapsulate and preserve thousands of samples of American-made cloth. The charm quilts in the Bresler Collection illustrate the range of fabric print designs and colors available in the last quarter of the nineteenth century. One, for example, contains a wide variety of late nineteenth century prints including rust-colored madder prints, black-and-white mourning prints, conversation prints, and turkey red calicos (fig. 8).[19] One hundred years earlier, fabrics for dresses and home furnishings were imported and expensive. American textile mills in the late 1800s finally produced an abundant supply of low-cost prints.

FOUNDATION PIECED QUILTS: LOG CABIN AND CRAZY QUILTS

Crazy quilts and log cabin quilts form a large sub-group of pieced quilts. Based on the fabrics they contain, log cabin quilts appear to have been most popular from the Civil War to the early 1900s. Crazy

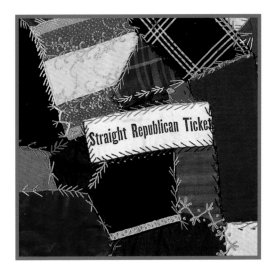

quilts were most popular from about 1880 to 1920. Unlike paper template piecing, the cloth foundation process is not so labor intensive and allowed turn-of-the- century quilters much greater leeway for personal innovation. Victorian crazy quilts, in particular, became known as America's "first art quilts." Made of pieces of silk and velvet and embellished with embroidered birds, flowers, and stars, these quilts were more than simple utilitarian bed covers.

Recycled textiles, including commemorative ribbons, were often used in crazy quilts. Accordingly, these quilts often contain dates, names or initials, and other clues about the making of the quilt. For example, the *Doll Quilt* in the Bresler Collection contains a printed ribbon with the words "Straight Republican Ticket" but offers no further clues as to the date of the crazy quilt (fig. 9). Typical motifs for crazy quilts include flowers, children at play, Japanese figures, and birds. Although some quilters might have traced their own designs for crazy quilt images, hot iron transfer patterns were also sold through art needlework catalogs distributed nationwide. Ladies Art Company of St. Louis, Missouri carried a full line of patterns for crazy quilt embroidery. The Vickery & Hill Co. of Augusta, Maine even published an instruction booklet with patterns for crazy blocks.[20] The Victorian *Crazy Quilt* in the Bresler Collection contains a wide range of silk and velvet fabrics. The quilt contains many typical motif-fans, interlocking circles, owls, a butterfly, a trumpet lily, and a small girl feeding a duck. The most unusual image is a group of birds sitting on a branch (fig. 10).[21]

Redwork quilts made between 1885 and 1925 are closely linked to crazy quilts because the same commercial embroidery patterns were used for both. The name "red" work refers to the turkey red floss used to embroider the design. Souvenir sets of designs or stamped cloth blocks were issued to commemorate turn-of-the-century expositions, such as the 1901 Pan-American Exposition in Buffalo, New York.[22]

Figure 10

HOWARD FAMILY.
American, 19th Century
Crazy Quilt circa 1890
hand-pieced and
embroidered silk velvet,
silk brocade, faux fur,
chenille, silk thread
Gift of Fleur and Charles
Bresler. 2001.38.11

EARLY TWENTIETH CENTURY QUILTS

The crazy quilt, log cabin, and redwork fads pulled the American Quilt in directions some feared might lead to its demise. By the early 1900s, crazy quilts were derided as garish and chaotic. Log cabin quilts were dark, thick and hard to keep clean. Redwork embroidered quilts were hardly quilts in the traditional sense. The American quilt had to embrace the new century and "modern design" or risk falling by the wayside.

At the turn of the century, *Ladies' Home Journal* offered patterns for "effective quilts of artistic merit." The magazine featured simply pieced, utilitarian quilts in one color and white—often blue and white or red and white. However, the January 1911 issue of *Ladies Home Journal* featured four appliqué quilts that had a profound and lasting impact on twentieth century quilt styles. Made by Marie Webster, a little-known, but talented quilt maker living in Marion, Indiana, these new quilts heralded in a new era for quilting design. The colors were softened; the designs were naturalistic, and the appliqué and quilting was exceptionally designed and executed. Ms. Webster's friends encouraged her to send one of her quilts to Edward Bok, editor of *Ladies' Home Journal*. Bok then requested she send others. As a result, four of Webster's quilts appeared as color lithographs in the magazine. The editors declared that a "new and artistic note has been achieved in these designs for hand-made quilts of applied patchwork. The aim has been to make them practical as well as beautiful."[23] A year later, four more Webster appliqué quilts appeared.[24] Webster's quilts essentially revived the center medallion format and elaborate quilting of the early 1800s, but, more significantly, her designs harmonized with the Arts and Crafts style of the early 1900s.[25]

Overwhelming response for her patterns encouraged Webster to establish, with the help of her family, a pattern making company. Her style inspired other designers, such as *Good Housekeeping Magazine*'s Needlework Editor Anne Orr, to offer similar patterns. Manufacturers, such as Stearns & Foster Company, closely copied Webster's designs for their Mountain Mist quilt patterns introduced in 1930. Quilt kit manufacturers produced similar center medallion designs using different floral themes.[26]

In 1915, Webster wrote a book on the history of quilts. Entitled *Quilts: Their Story and How to Make Them*, it became a source of information of antique quilts and patterns for the emerging quilt revival of the 1920s. In 1924, the Metropolitan Museum of Art in New York City opened its American Wing devoted to American art and crafts. This heightened the level of interest in collecting and exhibiting of American antiques, including quilts and coverlets.

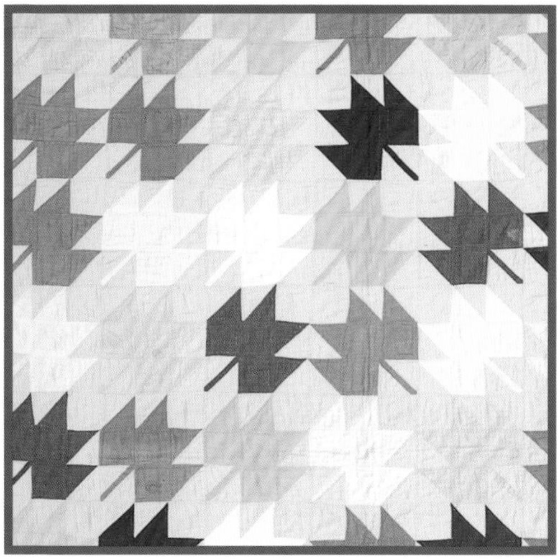

Figure 11
UNKNOWN ARTIST
Amish Maple Leaf Quilt
circa 1930
hand-quilted and machine-pieced cotton, rayon, cotton sateen
Gift of Fleur and Charles Bresler. 2000.62.11

Depression Era Quilts

As the Great Depression gripped the country in the early 1930s, the quilt revival was in full swing. For some, the hard times were relieved by quiltmaking. Others who had taken up quilting as a hobby in the 1920s were hungry for new patterns and new opportunities to exhibit their quilts. Quilt contests attracted thousands of quilt entries from both rural and urban areas. Enthusiastic quilters could purchase a pattern instruction sheet for ten cents. Sales of batting, fabric, and thread soared. Daily newspapers, farm magazines, and women's magazines featured regular quilt columns. The *Amish Maple Leaf Quilt* in the

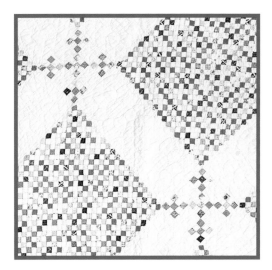

Figure 12

UNKNOWN ARTIST
Postage Stamp Quilt
circa 1930
hand-pieced and
quilted cotton
Gift of Fleur and
Charles Bresler.
2001.38.15

Bresler Collection might be based on a pattern the quiltmaker saw in a 1930s newspaper (fig. 11). A syndicated column described Autumn Leaf "as one of the patterns that has been handed down to us from the earliest days of quiltmaking. Its simplicity of construction—its practical quality—make it as much a favorite today as in olden times."[27]

Cotton fabrics introduced in the 1930s were light, bright, cheery, and belied the hard times. The *Postage Stamp Quilt* in the Bresler Quilt Collection contains thousands of tiny pieces of cloth popular in the 1930s (fig. 12). Some clothing manufacturers packaged cloth die-cut from remnants to sell as kits for pieced Grandmother's Flower Garden, Dresden Plate, and Lone Star quilts. Even appliqué designs for Dutch Girl and Butterfly quilts were die-cut.[28]

With low-cost fabrics and cheap pattern sources, quilt production increased dramatically during the Depression Era. It is, perhaps, because of these large numbers and the seeming homogeneity of patterns and styles throughout the nation that these quilts did not garner the attention of quilt historians or collectors until recently.

Research of late focused on 1930s quilt designers and their marketing techniques, coupled with interviews with quiltmakers revealed a much broader array of quilt styles and patterns. The *Phebe Warner Quilt*

Figure 13
UNKNOWN ARTIST
Phebe Warner Quilt circa 1930s
hand-appliquéd, quilted, and
embroidered cotton,
satin, wool thread
Gift of Fleur and Charles Bresler.
2001.38.16

Figure 14
SARAH FURMAN WARNER
WILLIAMS. American, 18th Century
Coverlet, Pictorial pattern circa 1803
Linen, with linen and cotton
appliqués, silk embroidery thread
The Metropolitan Museum of Art,
Gift of Catherine E. Cotheal,
1938 (38.59). Photograph by John
Bigelow Taylor © 1989
The Metropolitan Museum of Art

in the Bresler Collection is illustrative of this newfound information
(fig. 13). The quilt was purchased at a Sotheby's auction with minimal
information regarding its provenance—only that the quilt was found in
Connecticut. Stella Rubin, acting on behalf of Fleur Bresler, recognized

31

the quilt as a close copy of a famous quilt owned by the Metropolitan Museum of Art.

The original quilt was made by Sarah Warner Williams of New York City for her cousin Phebe Warner in 1803 (fig. 14). Using a center medallion style and *broderie perse* appliqué, the quilt illustrates the high standards of quiltmaking of the early nineteenth century discussed earlier in this essay. Amelia Peck, textile curator of the Metropolitan Museum of Art, described this quilt as follows for the museum's quilt and coverlet catalog:

> This bed cover is perhaps the finest existing example of an American appliquéd coverlet . . . . Its maker was clearly influenced by the central flower-tree motif common to the popular imported Indian bed hangings called *palampores,* as well as by the pastoral landscape needlework pictures often worked by young women during the eighteenth century.[29]

The *Phebe Warner Quilt* in the Bresler Collection was first featured in color in Rod Kiracofe's 1993 book *The American Quilt: A History of Comfort and Cloth.*[30] With colorful prints and a predominance of Nile Green for the appliqué stems and leaves, there is no doubt this quilt was made in the 1930s, but why would someone replicate such a complicated quilt and how would she have access to the original quilt?

Of course, the unknown quiltmaker might have seen the original quilt in the Metropolitan Museum of Art. In 1938, it was on exhibit at the museum following its donation by a descendant of Phebe Warner.[31] In 1939, the original quilt was documented for The Index of American

Design, a Federal art project of the Works Progress Administration (WPA).[32] Furthermore, the watercolor rendering by artist Margaret Concha resides in the National Gallery of Art in Washington, D.C. in an archive of 18,000 WPA watercolor renderings of folk art and antiques in public and private collections. During the 1930s, the paintings were exhibited widely to encourage support for the WPA and may have provided the quiltmaker another opportunity to sketch the quilt.

The quiltmaker's identity may never be known. In place of the initials "PW" on the urn in the original quilt, this quiltmaker has embroidered different initials "EK," possibly her own. This quilt was one individual's personal quest to celebrate a nationally recognized treasure.

DECLINE AND REBIRTH OF QUILTING IN THE TWENTIETH CENTURY

The quilting frenzy of the 1930s declined dramatically as World War II loomed on the horizon. With cloth production for domestic use greatly reduced, women recycled feed and flour sacks for clothing, curtains, tablecloths, and quilts. Women often took wartime jobs outside their homes. When the war ended and women returned to their traditional roles, making bed quilts was not part of the modern homemaker's duties, nor was there leisure time for making art quilts.

By the 1950s and 1960s, women's magazines and newspapers no longer featured quilt patterns on a regular basis. Those who continued to quilt resorted to quilt kits and patterns traded among friends. The few "new" patterns were actually copies of antique quilts in museums.

Quiltmaking was in the doldrums.

Ironically, the post-World War II "Baby Boom" generation rediscovered the American quilt and gave it new life. New Yorkers Jonathan Holstein and Gail van der Hoof were at the forefront of this mid-twentieth century rediscovery. Like other Baby Boomers, though they did not grow up with quilts, they were drawn to them nonetheless. Holstein explained the attraction:

> We became interested in the design and graphic qualities of quilts in 1968 and began then to collect those which worked best as 'paintings.' We disregarded all the criteria which had traditionally been used to judge quilts (workmanship, age, condition, regional or historical significance). Three years after buying our first quilt, an exhibition chosen by us from our collection to demonstrate the extraordinary aesthetic qualities of pieced quilts, was installed at the Whitney Museum of American Art in New York.[33]

The exhibit of sixty-two quilts entitled *Abstract Design in American Quilts* opened in June of 1971. The planned six-week exhibition was extended until mid-September because of a favorable response by New York's leading art critics. Today, the Whitney exhibit is credited with launching the quilt revival of the last quarter of the twentieth century and is considered by many as the watershed moment for the American Quilt.

Just as quilts fascinated Holstein and van der Hoof, so too did they captivate many collectors, including the Breslers and myself. The quilts we first collected possessed neither particularly fine craftsmanship nor provenance. They were simply enchanting material objects. As our collections grew, so did our curiosity about the fabrics, techniques, and pattern names our quilts encompassed. We read extensively and consulted numerous experts. Together, we have contributed to American quilt scholarship. We felt privileged both to own these quilts and to live with these quilts.

Between 2000 and 2001, Fleur and Charles Bresler gifted their 36-piece historical American quilt collection to the Mint Museum of Craft + Design. Previously displayed in their home, these works now reside in the galleries among contemporary art works ranging from the traditional to the "edgy." These quilts hold within their layers a wealth of information about the people and times in which they were made and offer a glimpse of the creative human spirit. For as you gaze upon a quilt up close and then step back for an overall view, you can come close to realizing our human-ness. These quilters, many anonymous, made extraordinary artistic works out of ordinary materials. Their work has become an enduring legacy, a timeless inspiration to us all.

1. Fleur Bresler, telephone interview by author, March 19, 2002.

2. For a similar roller-printed pillar print manufactured in England circa 1830, see Florence Montgomery. *Printed Textiles: English and American Cottons and Linens, 1700-1850*, Figure 371, (New York: The Viking Press, 1970), 325. Fleur was keenly interested in the technology of fabric printing and purposely sought out quilts that contained examples of early fabrics.

3. Though Fleur extensively researched *calamanco* quilts in hopes of adding an example, the Bresler Collection does not include a *calamanco* quilt.

4. Bets Ramsey and Merikay Waldvogel, *Quilts of Tennessee: Images of Domestic Life Prior to 1930* (Nashville, TN: Rutledge Hill Press, 1986), 57-63.

5. "Fancy Needlework," *The Lady's Book*, January 1835, 41.

6. Virginia Gunn, "Victorian Silk Template Patchwork in American Periodicals, 1850-1875," in *Uncoverings 1983*, ed. Sally Garoutte (Mill Valley, CA: American Quilt Study Group, 1984), 9-25; Laurel Horton, "An Elegant Geometry: Tradition, Migration, and Variation" in *Mosaic Quilts: Paper Template Piecing in the South Carolina Lowcountry* (Charleston, SC: Charleston Museum, 2002), 10-21.

7. See Lacy Folmar Bullard and Betty Jo Shiell, *Chintz Quilts: Unfading Glory* (Tallahassee, FL: Serendipity Publishers, 1983); Gloria Seaman Allen, *First Flowerings: Early Virginia Quilts* (Washington, DC: DAR Museum, 1987).

8. For a discussion of John Hewson printed textile panels, see Patsy and Myron Orlofsky, *Quilts in America* (New York: Abbeville Press, 1992) 57-60; 62-63.

9. See Gloria Seaman Allen and Nancy Gibson Tuckhorn, *A Maryland Album: Quiltmaking Traditions 1634-1934* (Nashville, TN: Rutledge Hill Press, 1995), 12.

10. See Ricky Clark, *Quilted Gardens: Floral Quilts of the 19th Century* (Nashville, TN: Rutledge Hill Press, 1994); Bets Ramsey, "Roses Real and Imaginary: 19th Century Botanical Quilts of the Mid-South," in *Uncoverings 1986*, ed. Sally Garoutte (Mill Valley, CA: American Quilt Study Group, 1987), 9-25; Nancy Gibson Tuckhorn, "The Assimilation of German Folk Designs on Maryland Quilts," *Antiques Magazine*, February 1996, 304-313.

11. For a discussion of album quilts, see Barbara Brackman, "Signature Quilts: 19th Century Trends," in *Uncoverings 1989*, ed. Laurel Horton (San Francisco, CA: American Quilt Study Group, 1990), 25-37; Jane Kolter, *Forget Me Not: A Gallery of Friendship and Album Quilts* (Pittstown, NJ: Main Street Press, 1985).

12. To read more about Baltimore Album quilts, see William Rush Dunton Jr., *Old Quilts* (Catonsville, MD , 1946); Jennifer Goldsborough, *Lavish Legacies: Baltimore Album and Related Quilts in the Collection of the Maryland Historical Society* (Baltimore, MD: Maryland Historical Society, 1994); and Dena S. Katzenberg, *Baltimore Album Quilts* (Baltimore: Baltimore Museum of Art, 1981).

13. Dunton, 104-105.

14. Bets Ramsey and Merikay Waldvogel, *Southern Quilts: Surviving Relics of the Civil War* (Nashville, TN: Rutledge Hill Press, 1998), 31-38; Virginia Gunn, "Quilts for Union Soldiers in the Civil War," in *Uncoverings 1985*, ed. Sally Garoutte (Mill Valley, CA: American Quilt Study Group, 1986), 95-121.

15. For a discussion of sewing machines and quilting, see Barbara Brackman, *Patterns of Progress: Quilts in the Machine Age* (Los Angeles, CA: Autry Museum of Western Heritage, 1997), 9-26; Suellen Meyer, "Early Influences of the Sewing Machine and Visible Machine stitching on 19th Century Quilts," in *Uncoverings 1989*, ed. Laurel Horton (San Francisco, CA: American Quilt Study Group, 1990), 38-53.

16. Wilene Smith, "Quilt History in Old Periodicals: A New Interpretation," in *Uncoverings 1990*, ed. Laurel Horton (San Francisco, CA: American Quilt Study Group, 1990), 188-213.

17. For a discussion of charm quilts, see Pat L. Nickels, "Charm Quilts: Characteristics and Variations, 1870s–1990s," in *Uncoverings 1996*, ed. Virginia Gunn (San Francisco, CA: American Quilt Study Group, 1996), 179-202.

18. *The Household* was founded in 1868 by George E. Crowell & Co., Brattleboro, Vermont. I wish to acknowledge Wilene Smith's extensive periodical collection, from which these two entries have been culled. Her findings although not yet published have already yielded important references to the origins of particular patterns and traditions.

19. For a discussion of late 19th century cotton prints, see Barbara Brackman, *Clues in the Calico* (McLean, VA: EPM Publishers, 1989), 55-96; Diane Fagan Affleck, *Just New From the Mills: Printed Cottons in America, Late 19th and Early 20th Centuries.* (North Andover, MA: Museum of American Textile History, 1987).

20. *Ornamental Stitches for Embroidery* (n.p., n.d.) in collection of author.

21. For a discussion of crazy quilts, see Penny McMorris, *Crazy Quilts* (New York: E. P. Dutton, 1984); Virginia Gunn, "Crazy Quilts and Outline Quilts: Popular Responses to the Decorative Art/Art Needlework Movement, 1876-1893," in *Uncoverings 1984*, ed. Sally Garoutte (Mill Valley, CA: American Quilt Study Group, 1985), 131-152.

22. For further information on redwork quilts, see Deborah Harding, *Red and White: American Redwork Quilts* (New York: Rizzoli, 2000).

23. "The New Patchwork Quilt by Marie D. Webster," *Ladies' Home Journal*, January 1911, 25.

24. "The New Flower Patchwork Quilt," *Ladies' Home Journal*, January 1912, 38.

25. Merikay Waldvogel, "Quilt Design Explosion of the Great Depression," in *On the Cutting Edge: Textile Collectors, Collections, and Traditions*, ed. Jeannette Lasansky (Lewisburg, PA: Oral Traditions Project of Union County Historical Society, 1994), 86-88.

26. Merikay Waldvogel, "The Marketing of Anne Orr's Quilts," in *Uncoverings 1990*, ed. Laurel Horton (San Francisco, CA: American Quilt Study Group, 1991), 7-28; Merikay Waldvogel, "The Origin of Mountain Mist Patterns," in *Uncoverings 1995* ed. Virginia Gunn (San Francisco, CA: American Quilt Study Group, 1995), 95-138.

27. Undated news clipping "Laura Wheeler Design Autumn Leaf Pattern 406" The Cincinnati Enquirer, Needlecraft Department, New York City.

28. Merikay Waldvogel, *Soft Covers for Hard Times: Quiltmaking and the Great Depression* (Nashville, TN: Rutledge Hill Press, 1990), 2-23.

29. Amelia Peck*, American Quilts and Coverlets in the Metropolitan Museum of Art* (New York: Dutton Studio Books, 1990), 16-19.

30. Rod Kiracofe, *The American Quilt: A History of Cloth and Comfort 1750-1950* (New York: Clarkson Potter, 1993), 182, 209.

31. Joseph Downs, "Four American Coverlets," *Bulletin of the Metropolitan Museum of Art*, no. 33. (August 1938), 180-82.

32. Margaret Concha, *Appliqué and Embroidered Coverlet* (#1943.8.2756) Index of American Design, National Gallery of Art, Washington, D.C.

33. Jonathan Holstein, Curator's Statement for *A Guide to the Exhibitions-Louisville Celebrates the American Quilt* (Louisville: Kentucky Quilt Project, 1991).

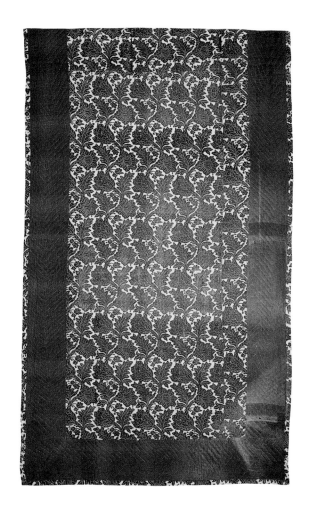

Resist Dye Coverlet

---

circa 1840
UNKNOWN ARTIST
hand-pieced, quilted, resist dyed cotton, linen, wool, indigo dye
99.25 x 60.5"
Gift of Fleur and Charles Bresler. 2000.62.6.1

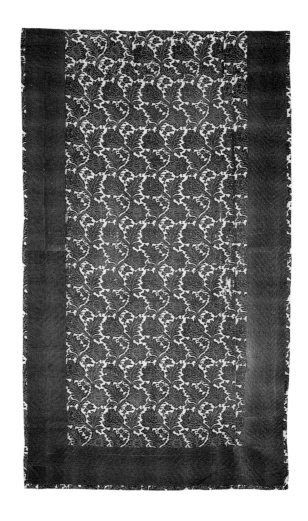

Resist Dye Coverlet

---

circa 1840
UNKNOWN ARTIST
hand-pieced, quilted, resist dyed cotton, linen, wool, indigo dye
99.25 x 60.5"
Gift of Fleur and Charles Bresler. 2000.62.6.2

Pillar Printed Chintz Quilt

circa 1830
UNKNOWN ARTIST
hand-quilted cotton chintz
103 x 108"
Gift of Fleur and Charles Bresler. 2000.62.8

Marseilles Crib Quilt

circa 1800-1825
UNKNOWN ARTIST
embroidered and quilted cotton
56 x 53.25"
Gift of Fleur and Charles Bresler. 2001.38.9

Cornucopia Quilt

circa 1830
UNKNOWN ARTIST
hand-quilted cotton
37 x 43.5"
Gift of Fleur and Charles Bresler. 2000.62.3

Hexagon Mosaic Quilt

circa 1845
UNKNOWN ARTIST
hand-stitched cotton
92 x 61.5"
Gift of Fleur and Charles Bresler. 2000.62.4

Bull's Eye Quilt

circa 1860
UNKNOWN ARTIST
hand-pieced, appliquéd, quilted, and machine-pieced cotton
85.5 x 79.375"
Gift of Fleur and Charles Bresler. 2001.38.13

Evening Star Quilt

circa 1845
UNKNOWN ARTIST
hand-pieced and quilted cotton
39.5 x 33"
Gift of Fleur and Charles Bresler. 2001.38.6

Nine Patch Quilt and Stencil

circa 1830
UNKNOWN ARTIST
hand-pieced, quilted, appliquéd, and stenciled cotton
83 x 92"
Gift of Fleur and Charles Bresler. 2000.62.5

Pillar Cloth Quilt

---

circa 1825
UNKNOWN ARTIST
hand-pieced and quilted cotton, chintz
49 x 40.5"
Gift of Fleur and Charles Bresler. 2001.38.5

Broderie Perse Crib Quilt

circa 1830
LYLE FAMILY
American, 19th Century
hand-appliquéd, quilted, and stitched cotton, chintz, wool thread, cotton fringe
45 x 38.75"
Gift of Fleur and Charles Bresler. 2001.38.3

Birds and Butterflies Quilt

circa 1850
UNKNOWN ARTIST
hand-appliquéd, quilted, and embroidered cotton, silk, wool, satin
75 x 84.5"
Gift of Fleur and Charles Bresler. 2000.62.10

Princess Feather Quilt

circa 1850
UNKNOWN ARTIST
hand-appliquéd, pieced, and quilted cotton
36.5 x 35.5"
Gift of Fleur and Charles Bresler. 2001.38.2

Medallion Quilt

circa 1861
UNKNOWN ARTIST
hand-appliquéd, pieced, quilted, and embroidered cotton, wool thread
43 x 43"
Gift of Fleur and Charles Bresler. 2001.38.7

Baltimore Album Crib Quilt

circa 1850
ELIZABETH FRAZIER
American, 19th Century
hand-appliquéd and quilted cotton
39.5 x 31"
Gift of Fleur and Charles Bresler. 2001.38.8

Album Crib Quilt

---

circa 1870
UNKNOWN ARTIST
hand-appliquéd and quilted cotton
42.5 x 44.25"
Gift of Fleur and Charles Bresler. 2000.62.2

Baltimore Album Quilt

circa 1852
CATHERINE BELL HOOPER
American, 1813-1881
hand-quilted, appliquéd, and embroidered cotton, wool thread
119 x 120"
Gift of Fleur and Charles Bresler. 2000.62.14

Album Quilt

circa 1850
UNKNOWN ARTIST
hand-pieced, quilted, and appliquéd cotton
75.25 x 86"
Gift of Fleur and Charles Bresler. 2000.62.7

Charm Quilt

circa 1880
RUTHIE STUBBS
American, 19th Century
hand-pieced and quilted cotton, chintz
89.25 x 87"
Gift of Fleur and Charles Bresler. 2001.38.12

Chinese Coins Quilt

circa 1900
UNKNOWN ARTIST
hand and machine-pieced cotton
64 x 64.5"
Gift of Fleur and Charles Bresler. 2000.62.15

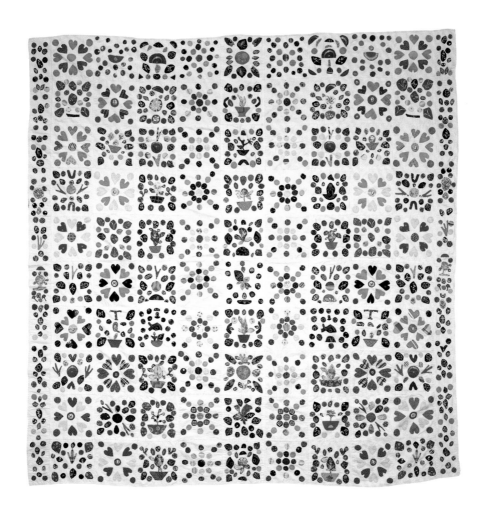

Appliqué Quilt

circa 1870-1890
UNKNOWN ARTIST
hand-appliquéd and quilted cotton
75 x 76"
Gift of Fleur and Charles Bresler. 2000.62.9

59

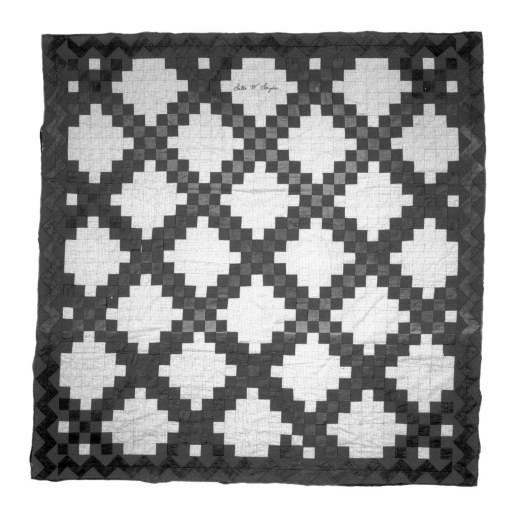

Irish Chain Quilt

---

circa 1890
SALLIE W. SNYDER
American, 19th Century
hand-appliquéd, quilted, machine-pieced, and embroidered cotton
77.5 x 75.5"
Gift of Fleur and Charles Bresler. 2001.38.10

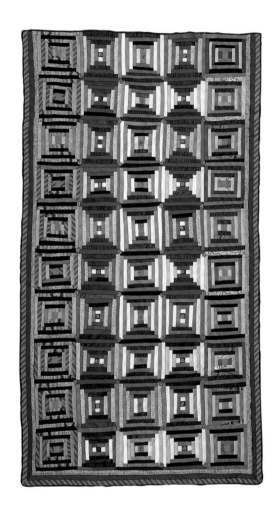

Log Cabin Quilt

circa 1870
UNKNOWN ARTIST
hand-quilted and slip-pieced worsted wool, wool chambray
70.25 x 38"
Gift of Fleur and Charles Bresler. 2000.62.12

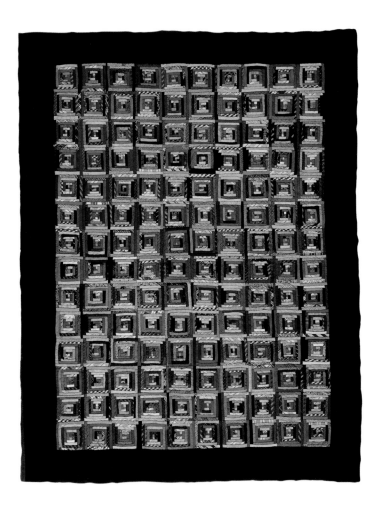

Log Cabin Quilt

circa 1875-1900
BASTEN FAMILY
American, 19th Century
hand-pieced and quilted wool, wool challis
56.5 x 44"
Gift of Fleur and Charles Bresler. 2001.38.4

Crazy Quilt

circa 1890
HOWARD FAMILY
American, 19th Century
hand-pieced and embroidered silk velvet, silk brocade, faux fur, chenille, silk thread
69.5 x 47.5"
Gift of Fleur and Charles Bresler. 2001.38.11

Victorian Crazy Doll Quilt

circa 1908
U N K N O W N   A R T I S T
hand-pieced and embroidered silk, velvet, wool
19.25 x 16"
Gift of Fleur and Charles Bresler. 2001.38.1

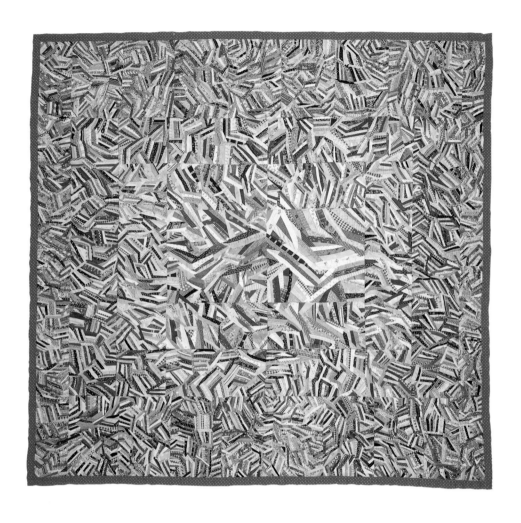

Crazy Quilt

circa 1900
UNKNOWN ARTIST
hand and machine-pieced cotton, flannel
74 x 77.75"
Gift of Fleur and Charles Bresler. 2001.38.14

Phebe Warner Quilt

circa 1930s
UNKNOWN ARTIST
hand-appliquéd, quilted, and embroidered cotton, satin, wool thread
76.25 x 70"
Gift of Fleur and Charles Bresler. 2001.38.16

Postage Stamp Quilt

circa 1930
UNKNOWN ARTIST
hand-pieced and quilted cotton
79.5 x 79.5"
Gift of Fleur and Charles Bresler. 2001.38.15

Diamond Quilt

circa 1928
E M M A   L A P P
American, 1885-1974
hand-quilted and machine-pieced wool
78.25 x 77.25"
Gift of Fleur and Charles Bresler. 2001.38.19

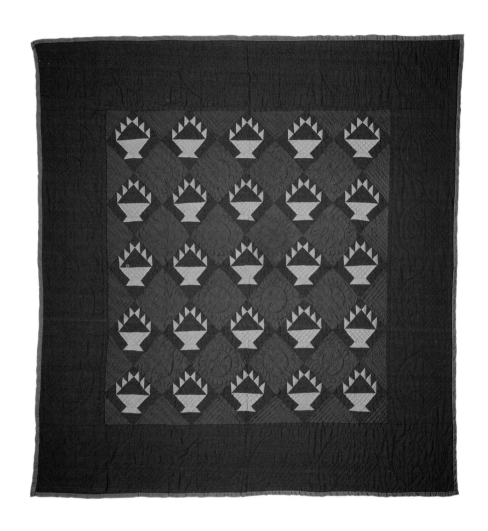

Amish Baskets Quilt

circa 1920
UNKNOWN ARTIST
hand-quilted and machine-pieced wool
84 x 70"
Gift of Fleur and Charles Bresler. 2001.38.17

Amish Star Quilt

circa 1925
UNKNOWN ARTIST
hand-quilted and machine-pieced wool
78 x 78.75"
Gift of Fleur and Charles Bresler. 2001.38.18

Amish Crib Quilt

---

circa 1920-1940
UNKNOWN ARTIST
hand-quilted and machine-pieced cotton, crepe
27 x 38"
Gift of Fleur and Charles Bresler. 2000.62.13

Bricks Quilt

circa 1920
UNKNOWN ARTIST
hand-quilted and machine-pieced wool, cotton
88 x 74.75"
Gift of Fleur and Charles Bresler. 2001.38.20

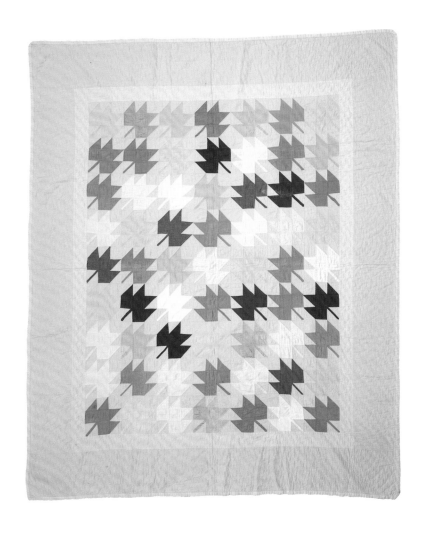

Amish Maple Leaf Quilt

circa 1930
UNKNOWN ARTIST
hand-quilted and machine-pieced cotton, rayon, cotton sateen
84 x 70.5"
Gift of Fleur and Charles Bresler. 2000.62.11

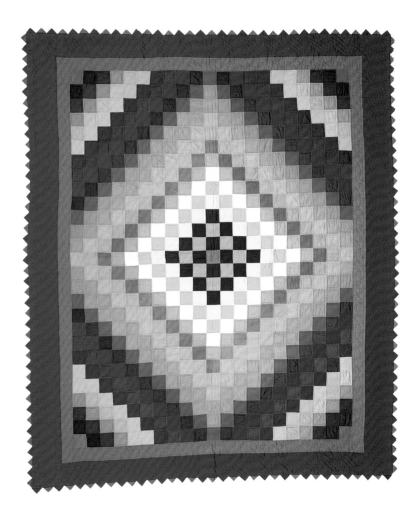

Sunshine and Shadow Quilt

circa 1980
UNKNOWN ARTIST
hand-quilted and machine-pieced cotton, polyester blend
93 x 76.75"
Gift of Fleur and Charles Bresler. 2000.62.1

GLOSSARY

Album quilt: a type of quilt in which each block is different; album quilts are often used to commemorate events such as a wedding or a birth of a child.

Amish quilt: a quilt style originating in the Amish communities of Eastern Pennsylvania and the Midwest; these quilts are usually made from dark, solid colors with ample use of black background and simple geometric borders.

Appliqué: the French word meaning "applied." Used in quilting, appliqué describes the process of sewing or applying colored cloth to a contrasting background fabric.

Backing: the fabric used as the bottom layer of a quilt.

Baltimore Album quilt: a type of hand appliqué album quilt which reached the height of popularity in nineteenth century Baltimore, Maryland; traditionally shades of red and green were used on a white background.

Batting: the middle layer of a quilt, traditionally made of cotton, wool, or polyester.

Binding: the material used to finish the raw edge of the quilt; the twill tape or cloth strip that is sewn around the quilt edges.

Block: the design unit or section of a quilt top that is usually square; it may be made of piecework, appliqué, or a combination of materials.

Border: the solid, pieced, or pieced band of cloth which frames the outer edge of the quilt or surrounds a center medallion.

Broderie Perse: a French term meaning "Persian embroidery." Also known as cut-out-chintz appliqué, *Broderie Perse* refers to designs cut from floral printed cotton and arranged on a foundation cloth. This technique was popular prior to 1850.

Charm quilt: a piecework quilt composed of many different fabrics in which no fabric is used more than once.

Chintz: a Hindi term (dating from 1614) describing exotic, painted, and printed calico cotton fabrics imported from India. Chintz fabric was often used for making draperies and upholstery.

Center medallion: a large central motif, typically of circular or ovoid form, surrounded by successive units or borders.

Comfort: a tied quilt.

Copper plate printing: a fabric printing technique in which engraved copper plates are used to print fabric designs comprised of delicate lines.

Cording: a technique which adds a three-dimensional quality to quilts; often, a string or cord is inserted between two parallel lines of stitching to create a raised design.

Coverlet: a bed covering, usually not quilted.

Crazy pieced: irregular shapes sewn to a square of cloth blocks, which are then sewn together to form a quilt top; edges of fabric shapes covered with embroidery stitching.

Cretonne: a French term for a durable cotton twill or linen fabric introduced around 1870. *Cretonne* was used for making draperies and upholstery; floral, paisleys, and pastoral scenes served as the subject matter.

Cut-out-chintz appliqué: (see *Broderie Perse*)

Embroidery: decorative stitching that embellishes and enhances quilt designs.

English paper piecing: a method of hand piecing in which fabric shapes are basted over paper templates and whip stitched together along their fabric edges.

Finger pressing: a technique for establishing guidelines in which a temporary crease is formed either by using appliqué or making seam allowances lie flat by pinching fabric between their fingers.

Foundation piecing: assembling a block by sewing pieces to a foundation of muslin or plain fabric; adding strength and stability to delicate or stretchy fabrics.

Log cabin: a type of quilt pattern in which narrow fabric strips, or "logs," surround a center square to form a block.

Medallion quilt: a type of quilt in which a central motif, surrounded by multiple borders, serves as the focal point.

Paper foundation piecing: a method of piecing or assembling in which fabric is sewn to a paper foundation with a printed block pattern in a specific order. This technique allows quilters to create elaborate designs; used particularly for miniature quilts.

Pieced work: joining pieces of cloth together to form quilt designs, usually geometric.

Quilt: a 3-layered fabric, comprised of two exterior layers of cloth which sandwich one interior layer of padding. The whole is stitched or tied together.

Quilting: in general, the process of making a quilt; specifically, the small running stitches that hold the three layers of a quilt together.

Roller or rotary printing: a technique of printing fabric using engraved metal cylinders.

Sashing: the strips inserted between the blocks in joining.

Set: the arrangement of blocks in a quilt top design.

Stipple quilting: a technique in which threads are stitched together particularly tightly and densely, in a somewhat random fashion, to ornament the large open areas of the quilt.

Stuffed work: the quilted or appliquéd designs to which extra filler is added to create a raised surface.

Template piecing: a method of quilt construction in which a fabric shape is basted to a slightly smaller paper template of the same shape and then joined to other units by tight overhand-stitching at the edges; frequently used with hexagonal and diamond shapes.

Top: the upper and outer layer of a quilt.

Trapunto: an Italian term, dating from 1924, meaning "to embroider;" a decorative quilting technique in which the design is outline-stitched in two layers of fabric, then padded heavily between to form a high relief.

White work: a type of quilt with a top of solid white cloth, usually featuring elaborately quilted and stuffed designs.

Whole cloth: a type of quilt with a top of solid or figured material, often three panels seamed together and quilted.

Adamson, Jeremy. *Calico and Chintz: Antique Quilts from the Collection of Patricia S. Smith.* Washington, DC: Smithsonian Institution, 1997.

Affleck, Diane L. Fagan. *Just New From the Mills: Printed Cottons in America, Late Nineteenth and Early Twentieth Centuries.* North Andover, MA: Museum of American Textile History, 1987.

_____. *Cocheco Print Works Collection from the American Textile History Museum*, Burlingame, CA: P & B Textiles, 2000.

_____. "Printed Cottons in Victorian America: Cocheco Manufacturing Company," *Surface Design Journal*, Vol. 9, No. 2, Winter 1984/5, 18-23.

Allen, Gloria Seaman. *First Flowerings: Early Virginia Quilts.* Washington, DC: Daughters of the American Revolution Museum, 1987.

Allen, Gloria Seaman and Nancy Gibson Tuckhorn. *A Maryland Album. Quiltmaking Traditions 1634-1934.* Nashville, TN: Rutledge Hill Press, 1995.

Atkins, Jacqueline and Phyllis Tepper. *New York Beauties: Quilts from the Empire State.* New York: Dutton Studio Books, 1992.

_____. *Shared Threads: Quilting Together Past and Present.* New York: Museum of American Folk Art, 1994.

Bacon, Lenice Ingram. *American Patchwork Quilts.* New York: William Morrow & Co., 1973.

Bassett, Lynne Z. and Jack Larkin. *Northern Comfort: New England's Early Quilts 1780-1850.* Nashville, TN: Rutledge Hill Press, 1998.

Berenson, Kathryn. *Quilts of Provence: The Art and Craft of French Quiltmaking.* New York: Henry Holt and Co. Inc, 1996.

_____. "Origins and Traditions of Marseilles Needlework" *Uncoverings 1995*, 7-32.

Bishop, Robert and Patricia Coblentz. *New Discoveries in American Quilts.* New York: E. P. Dutton, 1975.

Bishop, Robert and Elizabeth Safanda. *A Gallery of Amish Quilts: Design Diversity from a Plain People.* New York: E. P. Dutton, 1976.

Bowman, Doris M. *American Quilts: The Smithsonian Treasury.* Washington, DC: Smithsonian Institution Press, 1991.

Brackman, Barbara. *Clues in the Calico: A Guide to Identifying and Dating Antique Quilts.* McLean, VA: EPM Publications, 1989.

_____. *Encyclopedia of Pieced Quilt Patterns.* Lawrence, KS: Sunflower Publishing, 1979-1983.

Bullard, Lacy Folmar and Betty Jo Shiell. *Chintz Quilts: Unfading Glory.* Tallahassee, FL: Serendipity Publishers, 1983.

Cawley, Lucinda, et al. *Saved for the People of Pennsylvania: Quilts from the State Museum of Pennsylvania.* Harrisburg, PA: Pennsylvania Historical and Museum Commission, 1997.

Charleston Museum. *Mosaic Quilts: Paper Template Piecing in the South Carolina Lowcountry.* Greenville, SC: Curious Works Press, 2002.

Clark, Ricky. *Quilted Gardens: Floral Quilts of the Nineteenth Century.* Nashville, TN: Rutledge Hill Press, 1994.

_____. *Quilts in Community: Ohio's Traditions.* Nashville, TN: Rutledge Hill Press, 1991.

Clayton, Virginia Tuttle. *Drawing on America's Past: Folk Art, Modernism, and the Index of American*

Design. Washington, DC: National Gallery of Art, 2002.

Cleveland, Richard and Donna Bister. *Plain and Fancy: Vermont's People and Their Quilts as a Reflection of America*. Gualala, CA: Quilt Digest Press, 1991.

Cochran, Rachel et al. *New Jersey Quilts: 1777 to 1950: Contributions to an American Tradition*. Paducah, KY: American Quilter's Society, 1992.

Colby, Averil. *Patchwork*. London: B. T. Batsford, 1958.

____. *Patchwork Quilts*. New York: Charles Scribner's Sons, 1965.

____. *Quilting*. New York: Charles Scribner's Sons, 1971.

Downs, Joseph. "Four American Coverlets." *Bulletin of the Metropolitan Museum of Art* 33 (August 1938), 180-82.

Dunton, William Rush Jr. *Old Quilts*. Catonsville, MD: Self-published, 1946.

Eanes, Ellen. "Nine Related Quilts of Mecklenburg County, North Carolina, 1800-1840." *Uncoverings 1982*, 25-42.

Fox, Sandi. *Small Endearments: 19th Century Quilts for Children and Dolls*. Nashville: Rutledge Hill Press, 1994.

_____. *For Purpose and Pleasure: Quilting Together in Nineteenth-Century America*. Nashville, TN: Rutledge Hill Press, 1995.

Garoutte, Sally. "Early Colonial Quilts in a Bedding Contest." *Uncoverings 1980*, 18-27.

_____. "Marseilles Quilts and Their Woven Offspring." *Uncoverings 1982*, 115-134.

Goldsborough, Jennifer F. "An Album of Baltimore Album Quilt Studies." *Uncoverings 1994*, 73-110.

Granick, Eve Wheatcroft. *The Amish Quilt*. Intercourse, PA: Good Books, 1989.

Gunn, Virginia. "Crazy Quilts and Outline Quilts: Popular Responses to the Decorative Art/Art Needlework Movement, 1876-1893." *Uncoverings 1984*, 131-152.

_____. "Quilts at Nineteenth Century State and County Fairs: An Ohio Study." *Uncoverings 1988*, 105-128.

_____. "Quilts for Union Soldiers in the Civil War." *Uncoverings 1985*, 95-121.

_____. "Victorian Silk Template Patchwork in American Periodicals 1850-1875." *Uncoverings 1983*, 9-25.

Harding, Deborah. *Red and White: American Redwork Quilts*. New York: Rizzoli Publications, 2000.

Herr, Patricia. *Quilting Traditions: Pieces from the Past*. Atglen, PA: Schiffer Publishing, 2000.

Holstein, Jonathan. *The Pieced Quilt: An American Design Tradition*. Greenwich, CT: New York Graphic Society, 1973.

Hughes, Robert. Amish: *The Art of the Quilt*. New York: Alfred A. Knopf, 1990.

Hornback, Nancy. *Quilts in Red and Green: The Flowering of Folk Design in 19th Century America*. Wichita, KS: The Wichita/Sedgwick County Historical Museum, 1992.

Johnson, Bruce. *A Child's Comfort: Baby and Doll Quilts in American Folk Art*. New York: Harcourt Brace Jovanovich, 1977.

Katzenberg, Dena S. *Baltimore Album Quilts*. Baltimore, MD: Baltimore Museum of Art, 1981.

Keller, Patricia J. *'Of the Best Sort but Plain': Quaker Quilts from the Delaware Valley, 1760-1890*. Chadds Ford, PA: Brandywine River Museum, 1996.

Kiracofe, Rod. *The American Quilt: A History of Cloth and Comfort 1750-1950*, New York: Clarkson Potter, 1993.

Kolter, Jane Bentley. *Forget Me Not: A Gallery of Friendship Album Quilts*, Pittstown, NJ: Main Street Press, 1985.

Kraybill, Donald, Patricia T. Herr, and Jonathan Holstein. *A Quiet Spirit: Amish Quilts from the Collection of Cindy Tietze & Stuart Hodosh*. Los Angeles, CA: UCLA Fowler Museum of Cultural History, 1996.

Lasansky, Jeannette. *In the Heart of Pennsylvania: 19th and 20th Century Quiltmaking Traditions*. Lewisburg, PA: Oral Traditions Project of the Union County Historical Society, 1985.

_____. *Pieced by Mother: Over 100 Years of Quiltmaking Traditions*. Lewisburg, PA: Oral Traditions Project of Union County Historical Society, 1987.

Lasansky, Jeannette et al. *In the Heart of Pennsylvania: Symposium Papers*. Lewisburg, PA: Oral Traditions Project of the Union County Historical Society, 1986.

_____. *On the Cutting Edge: Textile Collectors, Collections, and Traditions*. Lewisburg, PA: Oral Traditions Project, 1994.

_____. *Pieced by Mother: Symposium Papers*. Lewisburg, PA: Oral Traditions Project of the Union County Historical Society, 1988.

Lipsett, Linda Otto. *Remember Me: Women and Their Friendship Quilts*. San Francisco: Quilt Digest Press, 1985.

Locklair, Paula W. *Quilts Coverlets and Counterpanes: Bedcoverings from the MESDA and Old Salem Collection*. Winston-Salem, NC: Old Salem, Inc., 1997.

McCauley, Daniel and Kathryn. *Decorative Arts of the Amish of Lancaster County*. Intercourse, PA: Good Books, 1988.

McMorris, Penny. *Crazy Quilts*. New York: E. P. Dutton, 1984.

Miller, Susan (ed). *Century of Quilts*. Des Moines, IA: Meredith Publishing, 2002.

Montgomery, Florence M. *Printed Textiles: English and American Cottons and Linens 1700-1850*. New York: Viking Press, 1970.

_____. *Textiles in America, 1650-1870*. New York: W. W. Norton, 1984.

Morgan, Mary and Dee Mosteller, *Trapunto and Other Forms of Raised Quilting*. New York: Charles Scribner's Sons, 1977.

Nichols, Pat. "Charm Quillts: Characteristics and Variations, 1870s-1990s." *Uncoverings 1996*, 179-208.

Oliver, Celia Y. *Enduring Grace: Quilts from the Shelburne Museum Collection*. Lafayette, CA: C & T Publishing, 1997.

Orlofsky, Patsy and Myron. *Quilts in America*. New York: McGraw-Hill, 1974.

Peck, Amelia. *American Quilts and Coverlets in the Metropolitan Museum of Art*. New York: Dutton Studio Books, 1990.

Pellman, Rachel and Kenneth. *The World of Amish Quilts*. Intercourse, PA: Good Books, 1984.

Peto, Florence. *American Quilts and Coverlets*. New York: Chanticleer Press, 1949.

_____. *Historic Quilts*. New York: American Historical Co., 1939.

Pettit, Florence H. *America's Indigo Blues: Resist-Printed and Dyed Textiles of the Eighteenth Century*. New York: Hastings House Publishers, 1974.

Pottinger, David. *Quilts from the Indiana Amish: A Regional Collection*. New York: E. P. Dutton, 1983.

Ramsey, Bets and Merikay Waldvogel. *The Quilts of Tennessee: Images of Domestic Life Prior to 1930.* Nashville, TN: Rutledge Hill Press, 1986.

_____. *Southern Quilts: Surviving Relics of the Civil War.* Nashville, TN: Rutledge Hill Press, 1998.

Roan, Nancy and Donald. *Lest I Shall Be Forgotten: Anecdotes and Traditions of Quilts.* Green Lane, PA: Goschenhoppen Historians, 1993.

Roberson, Ruth Haislip, ed. *North Carolina Quilts.* Chapel Hill, NC: University of North Carolina Press, 1988.

Robertson, Elizabeth Wells. *American Quilts.* New York: Studio Publications, 1948.

Rubin, Stella. *Miller's Treasure or Not? How to Compare & Value American Quilts.* Octopus Publishing Group: Rowayton, CT, 2001.

Safford, Carleton L. and Robert Bishop. *America's Quilts and Coverlets.* New York: E. P. Dutton, 1972.

Silber, Julie. *The Esprit Quilt Collection.* San Francisco: Esprit de Corp, 1985.

Sullivan, Kathlyn. *Gatherings: America's Quilt Heritage.* Paducah, KY: American Quilter's Society, 1995.

Schorsch, Anita. *Plain and Fancy: Country Quilts of the Pennsylvania-Germans.* New York: Sterling Publishing, 1992.

Swan, Susan Burrows. *A Winterthur Guide to American Needlework.* New York: Crown Publishers, 1976.

Waldvogel, Merikay. *Soft Covers for Hard Times: Quiltmaking and the Great Depression.* Nashville, TN: Rutledge Hill Press, 1990.

Warren, Elizabeth and Sharon Eisenstat. *Glorious American Quilts: The Quilt Collection of the Museum of American Folk Art.* New York: Museum of American Folk Art, 1996.

Woods, Marianne Berger (ed.). *Threads of Tradition: Northwest Pennsylvania Quilts.* Meadville, PA: Crawford County Historical Society, 1997.

Woodard, Thomas K. and Blanche Greenstein. *Twentieth Century Quilts 1900-1950.* New York: E. P. Dutton, 1988.

York County Quilt Documentation Project. *Quilts: The Fabric of Friendship.* Atglen, PA: Schiffer Publishing, 2000.